The Hobo Poet
A collection for all ages

by
Burnette V Mutter

©Copyright 2001 Burstone, LLC

First Edition

All rights reserved. Reproduction in whole or in part of any portion, in any form, without permission of the publisher is prohibited.

ISBN: 0-9679770-1-0

Library of Congress Number: 2001096770

Front and back cover illustrations by:
Mary Mutter DeYoung

Illustrations throughout *The Hobo Poet* by:
Mary Mutter DeYoung
Kelly Thorn Dulka
Wendy Johnson

Designed and Proofread by:
Graphic Liaisons LLC
Amherst and Waupaca, WI
graphicliaisons@excite.com

Published in the United States of America by:
BURSTONE, LLC
P.O. Box 15
Shawano, WI 54166
Phone: (715) 526-9277
Website: www.burstonellc.com

———————————————————*by Burnette V. Mutter*

Dedication

To my dear family and all my lovely friends that I met on the highway of life.
And to Fella, Tippy, Pal, and Laddie.

Contents

Dedication iii
Foreword vi

My First Garden 1
Autumn Returns 3
A Cool Reception 4
Our Beautiful World 5
Percy Blue Jay 6
Spring Things 7
The Country School 8
Christmas Is Forever 10
Happy Halloween 13
Autumn 14
My Best Friend 15
Tonki 16
It's Halloween 18
The Enchanted Hill 19
Winter In The Country 20
Welcome Spring 21
Wendy Wren 22
Wintertide 23
Forever Christmas 24
Tell Me 25
For My Son, Bill 26
The Smallest Pumpkin 28
Rollo Rooster 30
A Winter Scene 31
Happy Holidays 32
Dallman Schoolteacher,
Mrs. Marsh, Is Honored 33
The Brave Ones 34
Christmas Wishes 36
The Best Years 37
A Bunny Tale 38
Peter Puff 40
A Christmas Memory 41

─────────────────────by Burnette V. Mutter

A Christmas Wish 42
A Spring Note 43
A Pleasant Pastime 44
Sir Will 45
Autumn's Beauty 46
Thanksgiving 47
Christmas Memories 48
The Good Old Days 50
Bye To Summer 52
Christmas 53
"Salute To America" 54
The County Fair 55
Artist Of Fantasy 56
Autumn Time 58
I Wonder 59
Hollow Men 60
Snow Magic 61
Charms Of Summer 62
Thanksgiving Today 63
The Happiest Thanksgiving 65
An Autumn Thought 66
Ode To Winter 67
Robby Rabbit 68
Thanksgiving Day 70
Christmas Greetings 71
Santa's Helpers 72
The Beauty Of Autumn 74
Butterflies 75
Winter Magic 76
A Story - Old 77
Retirement HUMBUG! 78
Trick-Or-Treat 80
Our Greatest Possession 81
Happy Easter 82
The Good Life 84
Meet The Artists 85
Index 87
Laddie . . . . Back Cover

v

The Hobo Poet

Foreword

Burnette Veronika Mutter was born in South Milwaukee, Wisconsin, in 1914. She was the eldest of eleven children. Her parents were the late Peter and Clara (Bollig) Thorn. She completed nine years of education.

From 1933 to 1939 she worked as a nanny in Chicago. She also worked for one year as a waitress at "Dan's Barbecue," a restaurant located on Highway 41 in southern Wisconsin.

In 1940 she married John Mutter of Racine, Wisconsin. They operated a rented tavern located on Highway 100, "Mutter's Gutter," for two years in Oak Creek, Wisconsin.

In 1948, Burnette, John, and their two young boys moved from Racine to rural Shawano, Wisconsin. They purchased a small country store and tavern, which they operated until 1980, when they retired.

During her life, Burnette has traveled from the East Coast to the West Coast and from Alabama to Alaska.

In 1988, Burnette went on a six-week trip to Alaska with her sister and brother-in-law, in their motor home. She viewed it as the most breathtaking journey of her life. They attempted to drive the entire 1,422 miles of the Alaskan Highway, but had to detour using the Klondike Loop to Dawson City (a historical place from the gold rush days) as the Alaskan Highway was closed at Whitehorse due to rock and mud slides.

Some of the sights they enjoyed on the trip included: The Chateau on Lake Louise, Columbian ice fields on the Athabasca Glacier, and Snow Dome Peak that supplies water to the Pacific, Atlantic, and Arctic Oceans. They visited Chicken, Alaska, (the smallest town she had ever seen) and Tok (the name was changed from Tokyo during WWII) where they visited Santa Claus land at the North Pole and a church named St. Nicholas.

They spent several days at Fairbanks, taking in parks, museums, and beautiful mountain scenery; and especially the mountain scenery of the Mt. McKinley Range as they traveled to Anchorage.

Salmon fishing, viewing a flock of 200 Dall sheep on

by Burnette V. Mutter

the mountainside, and the devastation from the 1964 earthquake were some of the sights along the highway to the Russian River. The Portage Glacier was an awesome sight—one hundred feet of snow falls in this area in winter.

At Valdez they watched huge ships being loaded with "black gold" and luxury liners on cruises. Valdez was destroyed in the '64 earthquake and was moved and rebuilt four miles away along the coastline. They also visited a salmon hatchery and saw beautiful catches of salmon and halibut near the canneries.

Inspired by poet, E. A. Guest, who wrote "A Mother's Way," Burnette began writing poetry in the early 1960s. Many of her poems were printed in local newsletters and the *Shawano Leader* newspaper. Some were published in distant publications such as the *Milwaukee Journal* newspaper; *New Earth Review*, Murfreesboro, North Carolina; *Women's Household*, Seabrook, New Jersey; and *Good Reading*, Litchfield, Illinois.

Burnette received very little money for her work. A few poems afforded her $5. In 1992, *The Mature Times*, northeastern Wisconsin's senior monthly magazine, picked her poem, "Happy Holidays" (page 32) as an award-winning entry in their contest.

The real reward for her talent came from people who put her poems in scrapbooks, or, as one lady did, hung it on her refrigerator with a magnet until it became so faded she could hardly read it.

Burnette offered the poem "The Country School" to the Shawano County Historical Society where they displayed it on the wall. So many people asked if they could write the poem on a sheet of paper that the Society received permission to make copies available for those who requested them.

Through the years, many people wondered how a person with a limited education could write poetry. It appears that the extensive reading Burnette did in her early adult life afforded her the ample vocabulary to succeed as a poet.

She admits that her life was somewhat unorthodox and when asked how she wanted to be remembered, she softly replied, "as a hobo poet."

John J Mutter Jr.
Publisher

vii

—————————————————— by Burnette V. Mutter

My First Garden

I spaded up a garden
    and pulled out all the weeds.
I raked it, and I marked it,
    and planted various kinds of seeds.

A green thumb I don't have
    and a gardener I am not.
But I tended it and watered it,
    whenever the sun grew hot.

Every chance I had,
    I took a walk outside,
To watch my little garden grow,
    and I'd show it off with pride.

Somewhere along the way,
    something happened to my seed.
One thing is for certain though,
    I have a lovely crop of weeds.

The Hobo Poet

Autumn Returns

———————————————— *by Burnette V. Mutter*

Autumn Returns

Autumn came as quietly,
    as summer left today.
To start her work of artistry,
    on a lovely fall display.

She dipped her brush in dewdrops,
    her masterpiece begun.
Shades of red she gathered,
    from the setting sun.

Yellow gold from the Harvest moon
    and orange from a pumpkin crown.
The oaks stand tall and handsome,
    in leaves of satin brown.

The lush green pines for contrast
    and when she had this done—
A magnificent scene surpassed by all,
    to delight most everyone.

A Cool Reception

Outside my kitchen window,
    on the ground below.
A little Robin redbreast,
    is standing in the snow.

She looks so cold and lonely,
    and chirps the saddest tune.
I wonder if she's thinking,
    that she came North too soon.

I know a bird is very wise,
    and I'm sure she has a reason.
For she knows more than you or I,
    about the springtime season.

But I hope she has a nest nearby,
    all cozy warm and neat.
'Cause I never cease to worry,
    that she'll freeze her tiny feet.

by Burnette V. Mutter

Our Beautiful World

What's wrong, you say, with the world today,
    the condition it's in sure looks bad.
It isn't the world if you just stop to think,
    it is some people in it gone mad.

They have lost all respect for the laws of the land,
    and have no love or concern for their brother.
They riot and ruin, burn and destroy,
    and take what belongs to another.

What are they trying to tell us,
    what is it they want to say?
They can never solve problems with violence,
    nor bring peace to the world this way.

They take things for granted and take all they can,
    with never a thought of giving.
The world is so great with opportunities for all,
    but it does not owe us a living.

Someone's to blame for the trouble we're in,
    yet no one will say it is he.
We must all join together and help straighten things out,
    this job is for you and for me.

Let's pray to the Lord to give us the strength,
    to work with honor and pride.
And to keep his commandments we so shamefully shun,
    for these are the best rules for man to abide.

Percy Blue Jay

That cocky Percy Blue Jay
   I fed all winter long,
Would never stop and stay awhile,
   to sing a pretty song.

He stands outside my kitchen door
   and looks at me so bold.
And when I wouldn't feed him,
   he'd stamp his feet and scold.

He doesn't seem one bit grateful
   for a single thing.
Maybe that's the reason why,
   a blue jay doesn't sing.

———————————————*by Burnette V. Mutter*

Spring Things

Drifts of snow outside my door,
    have melted all away.
And spring arrived as usual,
    just the other day.

She sent a message to the birds,
    and a southern breeze.
She beckoned to the flowers,
    and whispered to the trees.

It's time to wake, you sleepyhead,
    your winter nap is through.
The gentle rains and sunshine,
    will tend and nourish you.

Soon fields and lawns will turn lush green,
    and butterflies appear.
Spring with all her magic ways,
    is the nicest time of year.

The Hobo Poet

The Country School

The old schoolhouse still stands there,
    now silent and forlorn.
Some windows in it are broken
    and the roof is weatherworn.

It used to be a happy place,
    for neighboring girls and boys.
Their voices filled the countryside,
    with a laughing, shouting noise.

We walked to school in those days,
    down country roads and lanes.
In winter's coldest weather,
    and stormy springtime rains.

We placed our coats and lunch pails,
    all neatly in the hall.
Then pledged "Allegiance to the Flag,"
    with pride we stood so tall.

We learned and worked together,
    and each one took his turn
Pumping drinking water,
    and carrying wood to burn.

At recess time we ran outside,
    and everyone had fun
Skipping rope and playing ball,
    or "Run, My Good Sheep Run."

Restrooms then were out-of-doors,
    but no one loitered there.
If it weren't for bees in summertime,
    it was the crisp, cold, winter air.

by Burnette V. Mutter

The teacher was most versatile,
    and she knew so many things.
She taught eight grades their lessons,
    to draw, and paint, and sing.

She was librarian and counselor,
    and our games she refereed.
She seemed to know just what to do,
    no matter what our need.

The best part of the school year,
    was the Christmas play.
We all sang Christmas carols,
    and each had a part to say.

A picnic in the summertime,
    was such a special treat.
Lemonade and ice cream,
    and tasty foods to eat.

These memories all linger there,
    inside the schoolhouse door.
Those happy days that we once knew,
    are gone forevermore.

I'm glad the school still stands there,
    for I often pass that way.
And I leave behind my daily cares,
    to recall a happier day.

Christmas Is Forever

I took a stroll through toyland,
    while shopping at the store.
And memories of years gone by,
    made me a child once more.

Christmas music filled the air
    and the shelves were stocked with toys.
There was something there to win the hearts,
    of all the girls and boys.

There were dolls of all descriptions,
    some baby dolls that coo.
Modern dolls in stylish clothes,
    that walk and talk for you.

Tiny dishes, an ironing board,
    and a dollie's bed.
A cupboard, and a stove,
    and a rocker painted red.

———————————————————*by Burnette V. Mutter*

Trucks, and trains, and airplanes,
   that really fly and run.
Skis, and sleds, and shiny skates,
   for all the winter fun.

Books to read and color,
   and some to cut and glue.
Countless games and puzzles,
   to pass the time for you.

It was hard to choose what I would like,
   from all those lovely things.
So I'll just wait 'til Christmas Eve,
   to see what Santa brings.

The Hobo Poet

Happy Halloween

by Burnette V. Mutter

Happy Halloween

Jack-O'-Lanterns smiling
    and some that wear a frown.
Peek at you from windows,
    'most every place in town.

Cowboys, spacemen, pirates,
    and a funny clown.
Gypsies, beggars, and a queen
    in a silken gown.

Goblins, ghosts, and skeletons,
    parade up and down the street.
Each one armed with a shopping bag,
    for tonight it's trick-or-treat.

Later at the magic hour,
    when the moon is full and bright.
If you watch real close you can see the witch,
    as she rides her broom tonight.

Autumn

I took a ride through the countryside
    and paused along the way.
To look at all the beauty,
    of Autumn's grand display.

The leaves on trees turned orange and red
    and some a shiny gold.
Amongst the green and stately pines,
    it was a picture to behold.

The brush and weeds add to the scene,
    in lovely shades and hue.
It's Autumn's way of saying,
    "A fond farewell to you."

———————————————— by Burnette V. Mutter

My Best Friend

I have a little girlfriend,
    just as nice as she can be.
I tell her all my secrets,
    and she tells hers to me.

On sunny days we play outdoors,
    and always share my swing.
When it rains we stay inside,
    to laugh, and dance, and sing.

We never, never quarrel,
    nor do we disagree.
I'd love to have you meet her,
    but—she's "make believe" you see!

Tonki

Tonki skunk was very sad
    and lonely as could be.
He walked along—his head hung low,
    what could be wrong with me?

He loved the other animals
    and wanted them to play.
But every time they saw him,
    they turned and ran away.

One day a little rabbit
    was caught in a snare.
Little animals all ran by,
    they didn't seem to care.

The poor rabbit cried,
    and called and called in vain.
Please someone come and help me,
    I'm trapped and in great pain.

———————————————— by Burnette V. Mutter

Tonki slowly walked along
    and just by chance came by.
He stopped awhile and rested,
    then heard the rabbit cry.

He hurried to the rabbit
    and broke the rope with care.
Then freed the little rabbit
    from that awful snare.

"Thank you Tonki," the rabbit said
    in the nicest way.
Then off they ran together
    and spent the day at play.

Now all the little animals
    come calling at his door.
Tonki is so happy,
    he's not lonely anymore.

It's Halloween

You better watch out,
    be sure to take care.
There's witchery brewing,
    in the cool autumn air.

The witch has been busy,
    all the goblins too.
Planning and scheming,
    new tricks to do.

Eerie skeletons dance
    and rattle their bones.
While spooks practice weird
    and blood-curdling moans.

Wee ghosts float about
    and "boo" with delight.
They are all set to haunt you,
    on Halloween night.

———————————————————————*by Burnette V. Mutter*

The Enchanted Hill

There's a high, green hill that I love to climb,
    on a balmy, summer day.
To watch the clouds form lovely things,
    as they slowly pass my way.

Some fuzzy bears do a tumbling act,
    and are funny as can be.
Then a fleet of ships goes sailing by,
    through a calm and azure sea.

Warriors bold on great white steeds,
    all armed with spears to fight.
A dragon fierce, who has puffed on by,
    then disappeared from sight.

This is my escape from a busy world,
    and the problems that come my way.
Soon I'll return to the high, green hill,
    to spend another day.

Winter In The Country

One marvels at the beauty,
   of freshly fallen snow.
And the drifts swirled high and sculptured,
   by the mighty winds that blow.

The firs are trimmed and bare trees clothed,
   in robes of ermine white.
Adorned with gems that sparkle,
   when the sun is shining bright.

A perfect work of art,
   done by the Master's hand.
Has turned the dismal countryside,
   into a lovely wonderland.

———————————————————— by Burnette V. Mutter

Welcome Spring

Lovely things are happening,
    now that spring has come to stay.
Sights and sounds all greet us,
    in a most delightful way.

Singing birds are building nests,
    in the trees nearby.
Ducks and geese in perfect form,
    go racing through the sky.

Everything looks clean and fresh,
    the grass is lush and green.
And dandelions with golden crowns,
    in clusters can be seen.

Crocuses have poked their heads,
    up through the rich, warm earth.
The budding trees in rhythm sway,
    rejoicing spring's rebirth.

Wendy Wren

Wendy Wren is back again
   and found her last year's nest.
Her happy song just seems to say,
   she likes our backyard best.

Housecleaning will be early,
   she has no time to spare.
Fluffy feathers she must find,
   to line her nest with care.

And when her tiny babies hatch,
   she'll cuddle them with love.
Then sing the news to one and all,
   from the treetops up above.

Her babes are always hungry,
   they keep chirping all day long.
And tho' they keep her busy,
   she finds time to sing a song.

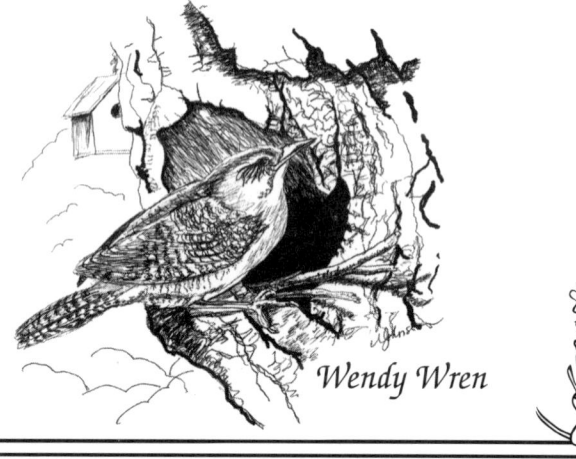

Wendy Wren

———————————————— by Burnette V. Mutter

Wintertide

Wintertime is so much fun,
   out in the countryside.
There are creeks and ponds for skating,
   and snow-covered hills to slide.

And it's great to make a snowman,
   in a funny pose.
With eyes of coal that sparkle,
   and a crooked carrot nose.

Singing songs on a sleigh ride,
   on a crisp and moonlit night.
Or building a fort in the meadow,
   for a friendly snowball fight.

Ski slopes in the distance,
   and trails across the fields.
For the latest thing in winter fun,
   the sporty snowmobiles.

But I'm a dreamer—this I know.
   So I'll don my boots and heavy coat
and finish shoveling snow.

Forever Christmas

I thought I wouldn't bother
    with a Christmas tree.
For there'll be no one home to see it,
    no one but Dad and me.

The children called to tell us,
    they had other plans this year,
And would send us each a present,
    with their love and Yuletide cheer.

But as the holidays drew closer,
    the spirit got to me.
I went to town and bought us,
    just a "little" Christmas tree.

I took out the box of ornaments,
    and hung a special few.
Some things the children made in school,
    and some pictures that they drew.

As I spent the evening trimming things,
    it seemed I heard the noise—
Of children waking Christmas morn,
    delighted with their toys.

This Christmas Eve when we light the tree,
    we will sit and reminisce—
Of the happy days of yesteryear,
    and the beautiful story of Christmas.

by Burnette V. Mutter

Tell Me

Where is the wind,
    when it doesn't blow?
Does it ever rest?
    I'd like to know.

Is it solid or hollow,
    and does it bend?
Where does it start,
    and where does it end?

If it's not in the sky,
    on land, or at sea,
Then where in the world,
    can that wind be?

For My Son, Bill

You have grown, boy, to a man so fine,
    I'm proud and happy you're a son of mine.
Your childhood days sped by so fast,
    but fond memories forever will last.
The fun you had when the summer came,
    riding your bike or playing a game.
Or just loafing around without worry or care,
    in jeans all patched and feet that were bare.
Your pockets held wonders and secret things,
    like turtles, and frogs, and a Lone Ranger ring.
Fishing all day with your brother Jo,
    swimming the river where the water was low.
Racing and running and making such noise,
    surely God made the summer for laughing boys.
You and your brother both loved to explore,
    the wonders of nature and the great outdoors.

by Burnette V. Mutter

I can see you yet on the path out back,
    with your dog, and gun, and old knapsack.
Your favorite sport was hunting raccoon,
    in old cornfields by light from the moon.
Late in the fall came the hunt of the year,
    the first time you went hunting for deer.
To get your things ready took most of the night,
    but long before dawn you were gone out of sight.
Way down in the swamp you took your stand,
    found a small clearing to survey open land.
Out in the field came this great big buck,
    you raised your arms slowly then prayed for luck.
Took aim and fired, he fell dead in his track,
    a beautiful beast with an eight-point rack.
Gee, you were so proud, do you recall?
    These memories, Bill, are the best of all.

The Smallest Pumpkin

The farmer sorted pumpkins,
    and set them neatly in a row.
The largest, nicest, perfect ones,
    were placed in front for show.

School left out and children came,
    their laughter filled the air.
Each bought a pumpkin of his choice,
    then took it home with care.

They carved and trimmed their pumpkins,
    then gathered down the street,
For the gala Halloween parade,
    then later on for trick-or-treat.

A lonely boy walked slowly,
    a tear was in his eye.
"If I only had some money,
    a pumpkin I could buy."

Just then he saw a pumpkin,
    that the farmer cast aside.
"I could never sell one small as this,
    no matter how I tried."

by Burnette V. Mutter

So the boy picked up the pumpkin,
   his heart was filled with joy.
This gift so very small,
   made him a happy boy.

He carved his pumpkin gently,
   and when he had it done,
He joined the crowd of children
   and everyone had fun.

They judged the many pumpkins,
   and children in disguise.
The smallest pumpkin beamed with pride,
   he too, had won a prize.

When Halloween was over,
   and all the children were at rest.
The boy and pumpkin wore a smile,
   this Halloween was best.

Rollo Rooster

I had a little rooster,
    with feathers pink and blue.
I never saw one like him,
    and I wonder now—have you?

He had green feet,
    his eyes were red.
A curly, purple feather grew
    on top his yellow head.

I called him Rollo Angus
    Alexander Tim.
Wasn't that a pretty name
    to give a chick like him?

A mixed up little rooster,
    he was funny as could be.
Instead of "Cock-a-doodle-doo,"
    he crowed "Cock-a-doodle-dee."

by Burnette V. Mutter

A Winter Scene

A snowfall came last evening,
   it didn't make a sound,
As it trimmed the trees in cloaks of white,
   and carpeted the ground.

The underbrush so elegant,
   in gowns of frilly lace.
The old dried grass and stalks of weeds,
   seemed dressed in porcelain glace.

The countryside looked beautiful,
   as it sparkled in the sun.
A portrait done so perfectly,
   to delight 'most everyone.

But the fantasy so lovely,
   just couldn't last I know.
'Cause someone out in back just yelled,
   "Come help me shovel snow."

Happy Holidays

There's a hum in Mama's kitchen,
    as she prepares for the holidays.
For the children wrote they would all be home,
    from places far away.

She will get her lovely china out
    and polish the silverware.
They haven't been used in years she thought,
    as she handled them with care.

She'll bake some bread, and their favorite cake,
    and some Christmas cookies too.
One night she'll trim and frost them,
    just like she used to do.

The tree to trim, and the manger set,
    she'll arrange it all just so.
And to add to all the memories,
    she'll hang some mistletoe.

by Burnette V. Mutter

Dallman Schoolteacher, Mrs. Marsh, Is Honored

We have come from places far and near,
    to honor someone we love dear.
Our teacher, Mrs. Marsh.

Most gracious and so nice,
    when they gave away the patience,
I'm sure she went there twice.

Some days we were naughty,
    and as trying as could be.
But she had a secret system,
    for kids like you and me.

She treated us with kindness,
    and praised us when we won.
She helped us if we fell behind,
    until our work was done.

She taught us to be truthful,
    and always keep in mind,
Respect for other people,
    and to our friends be kind.

We couldn't help but grow up good,
    with a teacher such as she.
So, we came today to tell her,
    we're as thankful as can be.

We wish her health and happiness,
    and the best of everything.
And many lovely memories,
    that dedication brings.

The Brave Ones

Yesterday a little boy,
    today a man so tall.
Yesterday the school bell rang,
    today your country called.

You set your books upon the shelf
    and put your things away.
Your childhood gone forever,
    you are a man today.

Do you recall when you said goodbye
    and slowly closed the door?
How proud you walked, they needed you
    to help win a war.

What thoughts went through your mind,
    when you left your home that day?
So young and eager and unaware,
    of the dangers on your way.

Did you cry? Don't be ashamed,
    great heroes shed tears too.
Once they were boys and all too soon,
    were men the same as you.

So take their hand, pray God for strength
    and when this war is won,
We'll thank the Lord for a land that's free,
    and the brave young men, their job well done.

With a silent prayer for the brave ones,
    who fell along the way.
They gave their lives to bring us peace,
    what a precious price to pay.

by Burnette V. Mutter

The Brave Ones

Christmas Wishes

It's a blessing that we celebrate,
    Christmas time each year.
It brings us closer to the Lord,
    and the folks we love so dear.

And it brings to mind the miracle,
    of the Christ Child's birth.
When herald angels told the news,
    that echoed 'round the earth.

Humble people gathered near
    and the kings from far away,
Paid homage to the newborn Babe,
    in the manger where He lay.

Today, as then, we praise the Lord,
    with songs of love sincere.
And we wish to all a Merry Christmas
    and a happy, bright New Year.

by Burnette V. Mutter

The Best Years

The playground is forsaken,
    the park and swimming pool.
By happy, laughing children,
    who have all gone back to school.

Their thoughts now are the serious kind,
    as they study day-by-day.
About the world around them,
    and why it is that way.

They learn about the oceans,
    and the mountains high.
The distance from the earth,
    to the sun up in the sky.

How many minutes in an hour,
    and hours in a day.
They learn to add and multiply,
    and sometimes take away.

About the different countries,
    and the culture of each race.
Satellites and astronauts,
    and flights in outer space.

So the park, the pool, and playground,
    will have to wait I fear.
For the happy, laughing children,
    until vacation time next year.

A Bunny Tale

Miss Becky Rabbit hurried,
    with a basket on her arm.
She had gathered eggs from all the hens,
    on Mr. Winkler's farm.

She stopped in for her order
    at the candy store.
And met young Silas Rabbit,
    coming out the door.

"Oh, Becky, something's happened,
    I have sad news to tell.
Old Lionel Rabbit has the gout
    and he's not feeling well."

Everyone knew Lionel,
    a rabbit kind and dear.
He colored eggs for children,
    at this time each year.

"Oh dear, what will we do?"
    cried Becky in dismay.
"No one to color eggs
    and tomorrow's Easter day!"

Becky Rabbit

by Burnette V. Mutter

"I'll help you, Becky," Silas said,
    in a voice sincere and shy.
"I've watched old Lionel many times,
    and I'll be proud to try."
"Thank you, Silas," Becky said.
    "Then we must work in haste.
I'll call in all my helpers,
    there is no time to waste."

Soon the helpers all arrived,
    they knew just what to do.
So they worked and sang in harmony,
    all the whole night through.

When morning came their work was done,
    Miss Becky bid them stay.
For a lovely Bunny party,
    on a happy Easter day.

A Bunny Tale

Peter Puff

I have a little kitten,
    his name is Peter Puff.
A playful little kitten,
    with fur of silken fluff.

I feed him milk—he likes it warm
    and when I have him fed—
He washes clean his face and paws,
    then curls up on my bed.

by Burnette V. Mutter

A Christmas Memory

I love to think of Christmas time,
    back in my childhood days.
When there was warmth and joy in giving,
    and life seemed easier in ways.

We thought our tree was beautiful,
    though oft times lean and bare.
But Mother was an artist,
    and she trimmed it with great care.

She baked and frosted cookies,
    several nights before.
Made popcorn balls and candy,
    that she hid behind closed doors.

For me, she knit a pretty scarf,
    and Dad a pair of socks.
Betty got a big rag doll,
    little Bob some wooden blocks.

On Christmas morn when we awoke,
    how happy we would be.
So thankful for our gifts and treats,
    beneath our Christmas tree.

Then all of us would go to church,
    and bow our heads and pray.
With love to baby Jesus,
    for it was Christmas—His birthday.

A Christmas Wish

I looked through my cards for
    one that would please,
A prisoner of war somewhere
    overseas.
The cards were all pretty and
    sounded so gay.
But none had a message I wanted
    to say.
So I put them aside and sat down
    and wrote,
A greeting to him in a short
    Christmas note.
We are getting things ready for
    the holiday,
And plan to spend Christmas the
    same old way.
Like the Babe in the manger
    'neath a lone little star,
We send you our love in a land
    way off far.
On Christmas Eve when we light
    up the tree,
We will all say a prayer that soon
    you'll be free.
And next Christmas day you will
    be home to stay,
To spend Christmas with us the
    same old way.

by Burnette V. Mutter

A Spring Note

Guess who came to dinner?
    A welcome, honored guest.
Dining with the snowbirds,
    was lovely Robin Redbreast.

She ate a while, then chatted,
    and told the news to all.
About the things that happened,
    since they visited last fall.

As she left she thanked the snowbirds,
    and wished them safety on their way.
For they will soon be flying north,
    now that spring has come to stay.

A Pleasant Pastime

I watched a live production,
    in my backyard today.
Birds of all descriptions,
    came to eat and play.

Purple Finch and Juncos,
    and the flighty Chickadee,
Siskins, and bright Cardinals,
    put on a show for me.

Doves and Hairy Woodpeckers,
    and several Nuthatch too.
Redpoll and some Grosbeaks,
    all a different hue.

I think the Blue Jay pretty,
    but to other birds he's grief.
He eats the best of all their food,
    then stands and hollers, "Thief."

Wintertime is not so bad,
    I don't mind the ice and snow.
'Cause I'm sitting here so snug,
    from the winter winds that blow.

by Burnette V. Mutter

Sir Will

I've read in books about a bird,
    who is seldom seen, but often heard.
I watched and waited for ever so long,
    but all I heard was his lonely song.
Late one day in the twilight sky,
    I saw a little bird in a treetop high.
He looked so shy and sat very still,
    I knew for sure it was a Whippoorwill.
I watched him awhile then he flew from the tree,
    and later that night he sang a song for me.

Autumn's Beauty

It is the changing of the seasons,
    summer has bid a fond adieu.
And autumn with her grand display,
    has set the stage anew.

She has cast her magic spell,
    all through the countryside.
Coloring leaves a brilliant hue,
    and all the brush that dried.

As you drive along the highway,
    it takes your breath away.
The beauty of each stand of trees,
    like a gorgeous big bouquet.

A painting such as this,
    I could never find.
So I'll store away these lovely scenes,
    in the album of my mind.

by Burnette V. Mutter

Thanksgiving

We are thankful, not just today,
    but every day all year.
That we live in this country,
    its freedom we hold dear.

We are thankful for our families,
    our homes, and for our health.
Our neighbors and our friends,
    we treasure more than wealth.

We are thankful we are spared,
    the ugliness of war.
And pray for men less fortunate,
    on a battle shore.

We are thankful that we went to school,
    and were taught to understand.
That God created for all man,
    this great and fruitful land.

Christmas Memories

I wonder what a child would say,
    if he could spend Christmas in my childhood day.
The toys then were pretty, but there were just a few,
    oh, how happy we'd be to receive one or two.

The day before Christmas held magic it seemed,
    and later that night—of toyland we dreamed.
Of little toy soldiers, a drum, and a sled,
    clamp-on skates, and a wagon of red.

Tops to spin and a ball with some jacks,
    a windup train on a little round track.
Play dishes of china and a doll made of rags,
    storybooks, and slates, and colored beanbags.

On Christmas morning we were so thrilled to see,
    a present for all 'neath our beautiful tree.
The tree was all green, just as it grew,
    some ornaments we made from pictures we drew.

by Burnette V. Mutter

Colored paper was cut and formed in a ring,
    then fashioned together with ribbon and string.
Popcorn was strung and hung with great care,
    to hide a few places that looked a mite bare.

Peppermint canes and polished apples that shone,
    cherries on wires, and tiny, gilded pine cones.
Candles in holders were snapped to the tree,
    and lit by our parents for us children to see.

Way at the top a wee star sparkled bright,
    to remind one and all of that first Christmas night.

I think I know what a child would say,
    he would rather spend Xmas as we have today.
With his 10-speed bike and mechanical sets,
    battery cars, and high-flying jets.

As for me—I am delighted as he,
    with all his marvelous toys—
And his flocked, shocking pink tree.

The Good Old Days

The old man sat in his rocking chair,
  his head was bowed as if in prayer.
But he was thinking of by-gone days,
  and how things have changed in so many ways.

He remembered well when they settled here,
  the vast, dense woods and the land to clear.
How he worked with his dad from morn 'til night,
  and sometimes later when the moon shone bright.

They brushed and cut, plowed and dragged,
  picked stones from the fields 'til their footsteps lagged.
Rails were split and fashioned by hand,
  to fence in the freshly seeded land.

When harvesting time came in the fall,
  and the neighbors all gathered was the best time of all.
They pitched in together 'til the work was all done,
  laughing and joking made their work fun.

He could still hear the whirl of the old windmill,
  that stood like a king on a lofty hill.
The creaking pump by the water well,
  and the welcome sound of the dinner bell.

Now as he gazed o'er the fields so green,
  he marveled at the work of the modern machine.
Life was much easier as progress made way,
  but the old man loved best the good old days.

━━━━━━━━━━━━━━━━━━━━━━━━━━━ *by Burnette V. Mutter*

The Good Old Days

Bye To Summer

Summertime was good to us,
    with sunshine and warm rain.
It gave us garden vegetables,
    and fields of golden grain.

Orchards full of apples,
    that were ripened by the sun.
To store away for wintertime,
    when the harvesting is done.

Vines of squash and pumpkin,
    in various shapes and size.
Some to trim for Halloween,
    and some for pumpkin pies.

Mums and winter asters,
    in lovely shades to see.
The final blooms of summertime,
    to delight both you and me.

by Burnette V. Mutter

Christmas

The countryside was calm and clear,
    and a star shone sparkling bright.
Just as it did so long ago,
    on that first Christmas night.

The miracle of the Christ child's birth,
    in a manger where he lay.
The greatest story ever told,
    we celebrate today.

Though years go by and things all change,
    and memories fade away.
His love for us is still the same,
    on this joyous Christmas Day.

"Salute To America"

United States of America,
 we honor you today.
For your refuge and our freedom,
 we bow our heads and pray.

People came from many lands,
 and settled far and wide.
They built their homes and progressed,
 in this land that grew with pride.

Let's keep your land so fertile,
 the forests tall and green,
And everyone to share,
 the lakes and rivers clean.

America so bountiful,
 stand proud, your flag unfurled.
A haven for all mankind,
 the melting pot of the world.

by Burnette V. Mutter

The County Fair

There's noise and a lot of traffic,
    and excitement everywhere.
As people come from miles around,
    to see the County Fair.

Farmers bring their animals,
    horses, sheep, and cows.
Chickens, geese, and turkeys,
    rabbits, goats, and sows.

Various grains and ears of corn,
    potatoes, beets, and peas.
Pumpkins, squash, and apples,
    and a buzzing swarm of bees.

Ladies bring their finest pies,
    cookies, cakes, and bars.
Golden loaves of bread,
    and foods canned up in jars.

Happy 4-H children,
    show their projects off with pride.
They worked so hard and did so well,
    how can that Judge decide?

I could never be a Judge, I fear,
    for I am really not that wise.
But, if by chance, they ask me to,
    I would award each one first prize.

Artist Of Fantasy

Someone drew a picture,
    on my windowpane last night.
A lovely fairy castle,
    was etched in frosty white.

Mountains high that reached the sky,
    in lines of perfect grace.
The leaves on trees and flowers,
    were daintier than lace.

It shone and sparkled beautifully,
    when the sun came out today.
But when I wasn't looking,
    it melted all away.

I think I'll stay awake some night,
    in hopes that I might see.
Just who it is that decorates,
    my windowpane for me.

by Burnette V. Mutter

Artist Of Fantasy

Autumn Time

It froze again last evening,
    the dew was crystal clear.
We said goodbye to summer,
    until the coming year.

The brilliant shades of autumn,
    seem prettier every day.
So enjoy the lovely scenery,
    for winter is on its way.

The trees in gorgeous colors,
    each weed the softest hue.
A masterpiece so beautiful,
    that only God could do.

by Burnette V. Mutter

I Wonder

Did you ever hear
    the crack of dawn?
And often times I wonder,
    does the dawn come
up like thunder?

If this is true,
    that it makes such a noise.
There would be no need
    for alarm clocks,
for little girls and boys.

Hollow Men

What causes men to let their hearts,
    grow cold with hate and greed?
A lust for gold and power,
    to be their only creed.

To sow the seeds of discontent,
    violence, and strife.
That grow to bloody, ugly wars,
    with no regard for life.

What good the harvest that they reap,
    and victories they have won?
They must someday account to God,
    all the ravaging they have done.

They stand condemned—these hollow men,
    who let their hearts grow cold.
Useless is their power,
    and worthless is their gold.

by Burnette V. Mutter

Snow Magic

A snowfall came last evening,
    and covered my backyard.
The scene it made reminds me,
    of a pretty, picture card.

The trees and brush so elegant,
    in their white and fluffy wraps.
The fence posts and my garbage can,
    are wearing stocking caps.

Some summer things and a few old toys,
    I forgot to put away.
An eyesore just a while ago,
    look like a work of art today.

And icicles hang daintily,
    like precious gems so fine.
To form a sparkling necklace,
    on my sagging old wash line.

I love the magic snow can bring,
    but I hope it doesn't stay.
My catalog for seeds, you see,
    came in the mail today.

Charms Of Summer

Summer is delightful,
    with its warm and carefree days.
Clouds as white as cotton balls,
    move lazily on their way.

Birds of every color,
    in the treetops up above.
Sing for all a serenade,
    of happiness and love.

Butterflies and busy bees,
    while away the hours.
In search of honey nectar,
    among the pretty flowers.

Trees and grass are velvet green,
    and the smell of new-mown hay.
Makes me glad to be alive,
    on a lovely summer day.

by Burnette V. Mutter

Thanksgiving Today

Thanksgiving Day at Grandma's house,
    has changed in many ways.
The horse and sleigh have been replaced,
    by the snowmobile today.

She's at the door to meet us,
    with a warm and welcome smile.
Dressed in her fitted pants suit,
    Grandma dear is right in style.

But the smell of turkey roasting,
    doesn't greet us any more.
Grandma gets her turkey,
    at the delicatessen store.

And the luscious pies she used to bake,
    are just a memory.
She picks them up when she's in town,
    at the local bakery.

The old cookstove and wood box,
    that stood behind her door.
Her kerosene lamps and featherbeds,
    are gone forevermore.

They call these changes progress,
    and make life easier, I agree.
But don't you wish Thanksgiving,
    was the way it used to be?

The Happiest Thanksgiving

by Burnette V. Mutter

The Happiest Thanksgiving

I had a little turkey,
    I named him Poncho Pete.
I pet him and I tamed him,
    and gave him corn to eat.

Soon he grew fat, so nice and plump,
    poor Pete could hardly wobble.
He strutted about so proud and smart,
    singing, "Gobble, Gobble, Gobble."

Thanksgiving day would soon be here,
    then Pete and I must part.
The very thought of losing him,
    nearly broke my heart.

Thanksgiving morning I awoke,
    and found a grand surprise.
My mom was baking ham,
    and luscious pumpkin pies.

I thought all day about the things,
    that I was thankful for.
Besides my little turkey,
    I could think of many more.

An Autumn Thought

Autumn is the final act,
    of a lovely symphony.
The trees and brush in color,
    are beautiful to see.

Like a rhapsody so perfect,
    there is nothing to compare.
The wind in various movements,
    adds to the graceful flair.

Birds in flocks each evening,
    serenade from lofty trees.
They will leave by early morning,
    at the bid of a northern breeze.

As they sing to all a fond farewell,
    and the dance of the leaves is done.
The curtain falls so softly,
    and fades with the setting sun.

by Burnette V. Mutter

Ode To Winter

When winter comes it's slumber time,
    for the earth each year.
Mother Nature lulls to sleep,
    all her children dear.

Snowflakes fall as softly,
    as feathers on a breeze.
They weave a blanket for the earth,
    and a cover for the trees.

She sprinkles them with stardust,
    and when her work is done.
A masterpiece of beauty,
    lay sparkling in the sun.

To rest awhile serenely until the early spring,
    then warm rains fall,
And the south wind calls,
    to awaken everything.

Robby Rabbit

Robby Rabbit hopped along,
   on a crispy winter day.
Before poor Robby knew it,
   he was miles and miles away.

He couldn't hear his mother,
   and his home was not in sight.
Now it started in to snow,
   and soon it would be night.

So Robby quickly turned around,
   and started to go back.
But the wind had played a trick on him,
   and covered up his track.

Robby stood bewildered,
   his heart began to pound.
Nothing looked familiar,
   and nothing made a sound.

He hopped up to some bramble brush,
   crawled in and made a nest.
He'd make a plan what he must do,
   then nestle down to rest.

by Burnette V. Mutter

But sleep was not for Robby,
    as he lay there crouched in fright.
At the eerie sounds of the woodland,
    and the darkness of the night.

The wind moaned thru the treetops,
    and the branches snapped and creaked.
A lone wolf howled in the distance,
    and an owl nearby would shriek.

If I had listened to my mother,
    and her wishes I obeyed.
I wouldn't be here lost, and cold,
    and so very much afraid.

He was wide awake at daybreak,
    but he thought he dreamed by chance.
For there sat Billy Snowbird,
    up above him on a branch.

I'll be glad to help you Robby,
    I will guide you to your home.
If you make a solemn promise,
    that you nevermore will roam.

I cross my heart and promise,
    and he thanked the kind old bird.
And Robby never, never, roamed again,
    at least I never heard.

Thanksgiving Day

We are thankful Lord, for many things,
    this Thanksgiving day.
For all things great and small,
    we bow our heads and pray.

We are thankful for our gardens,
    and fields of golden grain.
A lovely sunny day,
    and a gentle summer rain.

For all the pretty flowers,
    the birds, and butterflies.
A stream to fish, a shade tree tall,
    and a rainbow in the sky.

For the beauty of the autumn time,
    with colors bright and bold.
Our homes to keep us warm,
    when the winter winds blow cold.

For a twinkling star at twilight,
    when all our work is done.
A tiny baby's smile,
    and children having fun.

For a loyal friend to visit,
    and to share our happiness.
A failure, and a heartache,
    or a bit of loneliness.

For our country and our freedom,
    may it always stay this way.
These are some things we're thankful for,
    this Thanksgiving day.

by Burnette V. Mutter

Christmas Greetings

Memories of years gone by,
    and the folks we hold so dear.
Come back to us at Christmas,
    with cards of love and cheer.

It's the time of year to get in touch,
    with friends we seldom see.
To tell of all the happenings,
    and about our families.

All year long we're busy,
    with scores of things, it seems.
But at Christmas time we mellow,
    to recall our fondest dreams.

Tho' times have changed down through the years,
    with wondrous things, folks claim.
As I read my lovely Christmas cards,
    the verse still sounds the same.

Santa's Helpers

Alby Elf was different,
    from other elves 'tis true.
There wasn't a job in toyland,
    the little elf could do.

But he came to work each morning,
    and tried so hard to please.
The other elves were very cruel,
    they would laugh at him, and tease.

The elf was nice and friendly,
    kind and most sincere.
And when Santa heard, he sent for him,
    to care for his reindeer.

Alby was so grateful,
    and he felt so good inside.
To know that he was needed,
    filled his heart with pride.

He loved these gentle animals,
    and they soon were friends with him.
He fed and gave them water,
    and kept them looking trim.

by Burnette V. Mutter

Santa Claus was very pleased,
    and praised the elf with pay.
He built for him a tiny house,
    where the elf could always stay.

Santa Claus grew weary,
    as Christmas Eve drew near.
His list for toys grew longer,
    each and every year.

So he asked the elf to help him
    distribute all the toys.
And the bags of nuts and candy,
    to all the girls and boys.

Alby hummed a happy tune,
    as he loaded up the sleigh.
Then he hitched up all the reindeer,
    and they all swiftly sped away.

As they soared up through the sky,
    I'm sure I heard him call.
"God bless the boys and girls and everyone,
    Merry Christmas to you all."

The Beauty Of Autumn

Summer bid a fond farewell,
    and Autumn came to stay.
It turned the lovely countryside,
    into a colorful display.

The leaves on trees and underbrush,
    are a picture to behold.
In scarlet red and shades of orange,
    and a bright and shiny gold.

The mighty oaks with leaves of brown,
    and stately pines so green,
Add a touch of sheerest beauty,
    to this gorgeous Autumn scene.

by Burnette V. Mutter

Butterflies

The prettiest things in summer,
    are the butterflies.
They are all a different color,
    and some, a different size.

Velvet black and tones of brown,
    and lovely shades of blue.
Each one touched artistically,
    with a pastel hue.

I love to watch them flutter by,
    on a gentle breeze.
They dine on flower nectar,
    and rest on trunks of trees.

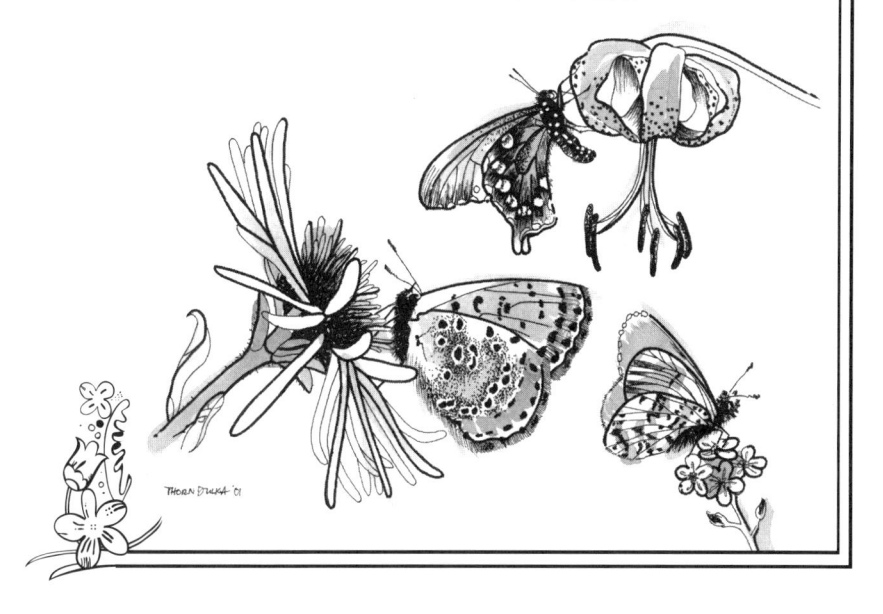

Winter Magic

I sat by my window and gazed with delight,
    enchanted to see a most beautiful sight.
The sun had come out so dazzling and gay,
    to brighten a crisp and cold winter day.
Soft snow had fallen everywhere,
    sparkling gems glistened here and there.
Tall pines in shimmering jewels stood prim,
    the oaks and elms wore sapphire trim.
Crystal hung from bush and pod—
    of milkweed, thistle, and goldenrod.
Diamond-glitter like tiny beads,
    adorned the brush and willow reeds.
Seemed each in turn would sway and nod,
    in humble prayer to our loving God.

by Burnette V. Mutter

A Story - Old

The little star shone bright,
    that night many years ago.
It twinkled all around the world,
    so everyone would know.
That a child was born in Bethlehem,
    in a stable bare.
And all who saw the little star,
    knelt down in humble prayer.
Shepherds from the hillsides,
    and kings from far away,
Brought gifts with love to Jesus,
    on that first Christmas day.
The world has changed and years gone by,
    since that first Christmas night.
But His love for us is still the same,
    and the star shines just as bright.

Retirement HUMBUG!

I can't wait 'til I retire,
    the old boy told his wife.
First thing I'll ruin the alarm clock,
    for it's irked me all my life.
I'll do a lot of fishing,
    and get out my trusty gun.
Polish up my bowling,
    just think of all the fun.

At last the day arrived,
    no time clock must he punch.
No driving in all weather,
    nor eating dried out lunch.
At first he thought it really neat,
    not a worry or a care.
Just loaf around the house,
    in his underwear.

by Burnette V. Mutter

He hasn't bowled a game,
   his gun is in its case.
His fishing gear and pole,
   all in their proper place.
He snoops around the kitchen,
   and is always in the way.
Sits before the TV set,
   and dozes night and day.

Helping with the shopping,
   is his latest vice.
Always in a hurry,
   and grumbling 'bout the price.
Retirement is great he says,
   but it drives his wife to tears.
'Cause he's finding out—
   What she's been doing wrong,
for over forty years.

Trick-Or-Treat

Ghosts and witches gather,
    for the Halloween parade.
Then later on they will spook about,
    and your neighborhood invade.

Ghouls and eerie goblins,
    skeletons, and hags,
Will greet you with an impish smile,
    and the biggest paper bags.

So have the treats all ready,
    for these tricksters of the night.
Or they will soap up all your windows,
    and give you an awful fright.

I know you will agree with me,
    when they finally pay their call.
That they couldn't have missed a single house,
    by the size of each one's haul.

by Burnette V. Mutter

Our Greatest Possession

Memories are precious things
    they are woven every day.
You store them in your memory bank
    where they will always stay.

Delightful ones of school days
    and all our teenage fun.
Happiness and heartaches
    or a victory that was won.

Memories of our loved ones
    bring laughter and some tears.
And the many lovely friendships
    we have gathered through the years.

Gold and silver men can seize,
    great fame can leave today.
But they cannot tamper with your mind
    and your memories steal away.

Happy Easter

Master Matthew Rabbit
    was as proud as he could be.
He had finished all the baskets,
    what a pretty sight to see.

Full of colored eggs and jelly beans,
    he set them in a row.
Then wrote a name on every one
    and on each he tied a bow.

Early Easter morning,
    into the homes he'll creep.
To hide a basket here and there,
    while all the children sleep.

Later in the day,
    when all his work is done.
He'll take a trip to Tennessee,
    to rest and have some fun.

He'll visit with his family,
    'til next springtime appears.
Then he'll return if you were good,
    as he has for years and years.

by Burnette V. Mutter

Happy Easter

The Good Life

An old man told me years ago,
    when I was just a tad.
To live each day as if it were,
    the only day I had.

To treasure every minute,
    for minutes have a way—
of slipping swiftly by,
    to form another day.

Accomplish something daily,
    to make your life worthwhile.
Although some days things all go wrong,
    try very hard to smile.

And take some time to visit,
    with a sad or lonely soul.
Help someone who falls behind,
    to try and reach his goal.

Pause each day and say a prayer,
    to the good Lord up above.
Count your blessings He has sent,
    then thank Him with your love.

The years have passed, now I am old,
    from my labors now I rest.
With memories of a happy life,
    and the thought—I did my best.

Meet the Artists

Mary Mutter DeYoung

Mary lives in the foothills of the North Cascade Mountains in the state of Washington, with her three college age sons, one dog, and two cats. Mary loves nature and enjoys gardening.

Mary's illustrations appear on the front and back covers as well as on pages: 12, 35, 57, 83, and 86.

Kelly Thorn Dulka

Kelly resides in Muskego, Wisconsin, with her husband, Jeff, and their three children, Vanessa, Natalie, and Carly.

She studied fine art. Her specialties include color drawing, painting, and stained glass design and construction.

Kelly's illustrations appear on pages: 9, 29, 51, and 75.

Wendy Johnson

Wendy is a former graphic artist who now resides in Galesville, Wisconsin. She dedicates her time to being a mother and homemaker. She is planning to write and illustrate a children's book.

Wendy's illustrations appear on pages: 2, 22, 38, 39, and 64.

A note from the publisher: Our family is blessed with artistic talent. Kelly and Mary are Burnette's nieces and Wendy is my step-daughter.

WOLF RIVER
Thank you John,
for putting this all
together for me.
XX ma

by Burnette V. Mutter

Index

Animals and Nature:
   A Cool Reception 4
   Butterflies 75
   I Wonder 59
   Laddie . . . . back cover
   My First Garden 1
   Sir Will 45
   Tell Me 25
   The Enchanted Hill 19
   Wendy Wren 22

Autumn:
   An Autumn Thought 66
   Autumn 14
   Autumn's Beauty 46
   Autumn Returns 3
   Autumn Time 58
   The Beauty of Autumn 74

Childhood:
   A Bunny Tale 38
   My Best Friend 15
   Percy Blue Jay 6
   Peter Puff 40
   Robby Rabbit 68
   Rollo Rooster 30
   Santa's Helpers 72
   The Best Years 37
   The Smallest Pumpkin 28
   Tonki 16

Christmas:
   A Christmas Memory 41
   A Christmas Wish 42
   A Story - Old 77
   Christmas 53
   Christmas Greetings 71
   Christmas Is Forever 10
   Christmas Memories 48
   Christmas Wishes 36
   Forever Christmas 24
   Happy Holidays 32

Easter:
   Happy Easter 82

Index

Family and Community:
- For My Son, Bill 26
- Our Beautiful World 5
- Retirement HUMBUG 78
- The County Fair 55

Halloween:
- Happy Halloween 13
- It's Halloween 18
- Trick-Or-Treat 80

Patriotic:
- The Brave Ones 34
- Hollow Men 60
- "Salute To America" 54

Remembering:
- Dallman Schoolteacher,
  Mrs. Marsh, Is Honored 33
- The Country School 8
- The Good Life 84
- The Good Old Days 50
- Our Greatest Possession 81

Spring:
- A Spring Note 43
- Spring Things 7
- Welcome Spring 21

Summer:
- Bye To Summer 52
- Charms of Summer 62

Thanksgiving:
- Thanksgiving 47
- Thanksgiving Day 70
- Thanksgiving Today 63
- The Happiest Thanksgiving 65

Winter:
- A Pleasant Pastime 44
- A Winter Scene 31
- Artist Of Fantasy 56
- Ode To Winter 67
- Snow Magic 61
- Winter In The Country 20
- Winter Magic 76
- Wintertide 23